MW01036664

The Art of
Law and Gospel

RJ Grunewald

The Art of Law and Gospel

ISBN-13: 978-0692733134 (rjgrune.com publishing)

ISBN-10: 0692733132

Table of Contents

Preface

One of the most dangerous problems plaguing the Christian Church is its failure to distinguish Law and Gospel.

As a Christian, I learned this distinction early in life, but it wasn't until much later that I learned that this distinction was unique and vital. As a Lutheran Pastor, I've immersed myself in the beauty of Law-Gospel theology, studying theologians like Martin Luther and CFW Walther. And as a Pastor, I've given my life to sharing this same message with the Church, because it's these two words, when preached in their fullness, give us exactly what we need.

God's Two Words

Martin Luther identified the importance of Law and Gospel when he wrote, "Virtually the whole of the scriptures and the understanding of the whole of theology - the entire Christian life, even - depends upon the true understanding of the law and the gospel."

These two words - Law and Gospel - are a gift from God. We need both words, but we need them for different reasons.

Without the Law, we are without awareness of our failure to be righteous before God. The Law tells us what to do. It sets the standard. And because the standard is high, it also highlights our shortcomings. It shines a light on our failures. The Bible makes it clear what we should be doing and how we should be living. It's also clear that God's people have don't have a very good history of being very good people.

The Law, in one sense, is the bad news. Any part of scripture that demands obedience, perfection, or tells us what we must do – this is the Law. Any part of scripture that describes our failure to follow the Law, this is also Law.

The Law's purpose is always to drive us towards repentance. The Law makes us desperately aware that we need a Savior.

We hear this from Paul when he states:

"None is righteous, no, not one;
    no one understands;
    no one seeks for God.
All have turned aside; together they have become worthless;
    no one does good,
    not even one." - Romans 3:10-12

Without the Gospel, however, bad news is just bad news.

The Gospel is the rest of the gift that is the perfect partner to the Law. The Gospel is the word that doesn't leave us without hope, but instead proclaims a message of rescue. The Gospel tells us what has been done for us. The Gospel reminds us that it doesn't matter how screwed up we are, because Jesus took our place on the cross. The Gospel tells us that by

His death and resurrection our sins are forgiven.

Paul shares the hope of the Gospel for us in Romans:

"No, in all these things we are more than conquerors through him who loved us. For I am sure that neither death nor life, nor angels nor rulers, nor things present nor things to come, nor powers, nor height nor depth, nor anything else in all creation, will be able to separate us from the love of God in Christ Jesus our Lord." - Romans 8:37-39

While the Law is all about what we must do and what we fail to do, the Gospel is all about what has been done for us. The Gospel declares that the perfect righteousness of Christ has been given to us.

These two words, Law and Gospel, are central to the message of Christianity. These two words are a message that Christianity has routinely forgotten, confused, and misapplied.

One of my favorite books about Law & Gospel states this:

"Christianity now is in crisis, and a large part because people have marketed it as a religion of good people getting better, when in fact it is religion a bad people coping with their failure to be good." - David Zahl[1]

When we have a clear understanding of God's Law and God's Gospel, this problem is eliminated.

A clear understanding of Law and Gospel makes us acutely aware of our own sin problem and in awe of God's grace. A proper understanding of God's law eliminates self-righteousness and pops inflated egos. And a proper understanding of God's promises gives us hope when we have nothing to hope in, joy when everything is falling apart, and grace when we deserve punishment.

Christians, including preachers, routinely confuse the Law and Gospel, misapplying both. Confusion results: Some needlessly suffer under a burdened conscience as they live under the crushing weight of the Law, while others dismiss the Law (unrepentant

---

[1] *Law & Gospel: A Theology for Sinners and Saints* by David Zahl, Mockingbird Ministries, 21. This is one of the best books on Law & Gospel available.

sinners) and ignorantly bask in grace they find outside of Christ's work on their behalf.

It's my hope that this book will help you become an artist skilled in distinguishing Law and Gospel, knowing that it is God's Law that always leads you to God's Grace.

The Art of Law & Gospel

Chapter 1

Have you ever experienced a film that ended too soon? The credits roll but you wanted more. There were questions left unanswered. Issues unresolved.

We crave closure. We want neat and tidy packages. We need to know what happened.

When movies end too soon, we wonder: Did the couple stay together? Did the good guy live? Did the bad guy get his? Did she ever find him?

Good storytellers have the ability create compelling stories while still holding back. In movies, writers, producers and editors continuously craft the film to keep viewers engaged and wondering what will happen next. Tension is built and released in a calculated manner. One difference between a good storyteller and a bad one is how they build and release tension.

The same is true for theologians.

Good theologians know when to increase the tension of the Law and when to release it by sharing the Gospel.

Did Jesus Know His Own Theology?

A rich, young man asked Jesus a seemingly simple theological question when he said, "Teacher, what must I do to inherit eternal life?"[2]

---

[2] Matthew 19:16-22, Mark 10:17-31, Luke 18:18-30

Jesus responded, "You know the commandments: Don't murder, don't commit adultery, don't steal…"

This is one of those places in the Bible where my good theological training makes me freak out. Jesus answered the question wrong. Luther would have even argued the answer was wrong!

What are we supposed to do with the theological issue that Jesus created when his answer to, "How do I inherit eternal life?" is a list of commands?

Did Jesus forget about grace?

Jesus showed his artistry as a theologian. Jesus knew exactly what he was doing when he delivered his answer. Jesus created an unresolved tension in this powerful scene.

The young man believed that he had kept the commandments since he was a young boy. Jesus seemingly ignored the young man's arrogance at his ability to follow the law and responded, "Go, sell everything you have and give to the poor, and you will have treasure in heaven."

And the rich, young man walked away. Sad.

And that was the end. The credits rolled. The house lights came up. The story was done.

Where's the closure? What's the rest of the story.

Jesus didn't chase after the rich, young ruler to clarify. Jesus said, "Give away all your stuff," and the young man left.

The End.

Not even close.

As we share the message of the Scriptures, we have the same difficult choice that Jesus faced with the rich, young man. What words do we share? If the Bible is a book of two words: Law and Gospel, the great art for the Christian is distinguishing Law and Gospel in the midst of spiritual conversations. It requires skill to discern when to build the tension in order to point someone toward repentance, and when to release the tension so one might rest in the grace of Jesus.

When do we share the words that expose the sin and condemn the sinner?

When do we share the words that offer grace and forgiveness and life to that same person?

The rich, young ruler was a bit arrogant in judging his ability to keep the Law and he needed to hear a word that would bring him back to reality and realize his need for grace. Neither his money nor his obedience entitle him to a life of grace and forgiveness. His pride must be killed in order that he might be given life.

The Law shatters the self-made delusions about the goodness we offer and leaves us broken with nowhere to turn but the cross.

The young man's response to Jesus's words wasn't surprising. In fact it's all too common a response even centuries later. Christianity, numerically speaking, is in a decline. Everyday people are walking away from grace. Many walk away like the Rich Man, arrogant enough to believe that they are good enough on their own.

At this point, Jesus made an important decision. Jesus let the story end. And that was really the end. There is no follow up with this man ... no personal visits, phone calls, e-mails or texts that offer grace. The final scene was the lingering sting of the Law.

Jesus embraced the unresolved tension by not sharing grace so that the law might linger and do its work.

The disciples on the other hand responded much differently to Jesus' conversation with the young man.

Jesus' preaching of Law led the disciples to ask the question, "Well, who then can be saved?"

This is the point.

The law did its work for the disciples; they recognized their inability to measure up to God's demands. The disciples felt the screws tighten. They felt the pressure. They knew that what they had to offer would never be enough.

So the disciples needed a different word. The disciples didn't need words that condemned. They didn't need more rules and laws. They didn't need "Seven Steps to a Life of Discipleship." They needed the Gospel. They needed the word that brings life.

The disciple's word is the other reason that we find so many walking away from the Church. While many walk away thinking their good and don't need grace, countless others have given up on the Church because they never heard this other word. They heard law and condemnation enough that it left them bloodied and bruised, but they were never offered the hope of the Gospel. They were driven to repentance and then kicked while they were down.

The Art of Sharing God's Two Words

You know the rhyme, "Sticks and stones may break my bones, but words will never hurt me." As adults, we know that just isn't true. Words do hurt. Life has taught us that words have far more power than that childhood rhyme suggests.

Words have the power to create and destroy; to kill and give life. The good news is that God's words always lead to resurrection. "Even when we were dead in our trespasses, [God] made us alive together with Christ - by grace you have been saved."[3]

Suppose a friend asks a simple, yet loaded question, "Is abortion a sin?" For some this question has an easy answer. However, when we start to discern whether we speak Law or Gospel, the conversation might instead dig a little deeper before giving the easy answer. As you talk, you may soon find out that this person isn't asking because she's trying to determine your political stance but because she's had an abortion. She is overwhelmed with guilt, and has been beaten up by Christian friends who unknowingly told her how evil her decision was.

The initial "right" answer might seem initially clear, but what she needed to hear might be

---

[3] Ephesians 2:5

completely different. She already was convicted and burdened because of the Law, she needed words that would give life. She needed the Gospel.

When the Law drives the sinner to repentance, the Gospel speaks words of hope. When the Law kills, the Gospel makes us alive. When the disciples ask, "Who then can be saved?" The Gospel comes in and says, "It is Jesus who saves."

The great theologian CFW Walther described the art of Law and Gospel by saying, "Rightly distinguishing the Law and the Gospel is the most difficult and the highest art of Christians in general and of theologians in particular. It is taught only by the Holy Spirit in the school of experience."[4]

We have a responsibility to use words wisely. Words have the power to correct those who live like there is no law. And they have the power to set free those who have been enslaved by sin.

---

[4] Thesis III in CFW Walther's *The Proper Distinction Between Law and Gospel.*

Speaking God's two words is an art. There is tension that we wrestle with as Christians when we share God's word. Which words do we speak? Law or Gospel? This tension is what prompts Walther to suggest this as the "most difficult and highest art." This tension makes Uncle Ben's words to Peter Parker (Spider-man) prophetic, "With great power comes great responsibility."

Whether speaking as parents, preachers, or as friends, speaking Law and Gospel is an art. It takes an artist to determine when to stop and when to keep pushing. It requires an artist to know how to build the tension and when to release that tension. And it takes an artist to discern, what words does this person need to hear right now?

Law… or Gospel?

The Law

"The Law reveals guilt, fills the conscience with terror, and drives men to despair."

Martin Luther

The Good News About the Bad News

Chapter 2

The Law gets a bad rep.

There is certainly a negative component to the Law. The work of the Law is very different than the work of the Gospel. If the Gospel's work is to revive, the Law's work is to kill. If the Gospel's work is to cover over sin, the Law's work is to expose sin. If the Gospel is the Good News, the Law is the Bad News.

Despite the negative function of the Law, the Law is not bad. The Law is good even when it makes us feel bad. Even when the Law functions for the purpose of exposing our sin, it does not exist for the sake of your exposure.

The end goal of the Law is always the Gospel.

The Hammer in the Hand of an Artist

In 1501, a young man by the name of Michelangelo began to destroy a valuable slab of marble. He cut, he hammered, and he carved, leaving piece after piece of valuable marble on the ground to be swept away. For months upon months, Michelangelo used the destructive force of the hammer to get rid of extra rock.

Cutting, carving, and hammering a valuable piece of marble is a bad idea. A hammer is a tool of destruction. Unless that cutting, carving, and hammering is done by the hands of an artist.

The Law is a hammer in the hands of the Master Artist - who is working on many individual masterpieces, one of which is you.

In Ephesians Paul writes, "For we are his workmanship, created in Christ Jesus for good works." One of the tools in the belt of the Master Artist is the Law that hammers, cuts, and carves in order that the Gospel might reveal a new creation.

At times the hammer swings swiftly and strongly. The hammer swings with force in order to clear away as much marble as possible. The hammer swings accusing our conscience while smashing our pride and arrogance. The hammer swings to convict the sinner. The Law swings with force to reveal what we really look like. It shatters our self-made image. When we see God's work, we realize we aren't as good as we think we are. It cuts away the excess helping us realize that we can't measure up to God's demands.

At other times, the hammer is more like a wooden mallet, gently exposing our sins and failures. The mallet smooths out the rough edges. It gently causes you to look at yourself and ask: What kind of husband am I? What kind of neighbor or coworker am I? What kind of friend am I?

The questions do the work of the Law. They continue to reveal what we really look like - that we are often more a piece of work than a work of art.

Notice the demands the Law makes. These are good things. The Law isn't bad.

"Be a better husband" is Law. It's good. It's important. But it's still Law.

The Law always accuses.

For example, "Be a better husband."

If you are a crummy husband, you're going to feel guilty when I tell you to be a better husband. If you fought with your wife this morning, you're going to think of all the ways you should've handled that situation differently. If you had a marriage that ended poorly, you're going to be filled with regret.

"Be a better husband," immediately exposes your failures. This hammer might swing in harshly making you feel like you've been punched in the chest with guilt. Or it might gently tap away reminding you of conversations or attitudes, calling you to something better.

Paul writes in 2 Corinthians 5:17, "Therefore, if anyone is in Christ, he is a new creation. The old has passed away; behold, the new has come." The new creation comes with the passing of the old. The destruction of the old materials leaves a masterpiece rising above the debris. The figurative death that comes at the hands of the Law is followed by the resurrection that comes in the beauty of the Gospel.

This is why Herman Stuempfle in *Preaching Law and Gospel* said, "the Law is never terminal."[5]

When Michelangelo began cutting, carving, and hammering a chunk of marble, his goal was never to destroy the rock. His goal was completed in 1504, the masterpiece sculpture, David. The Law is never the end goal. The Law always exists for the masterpiece that comes after by the work of the Gospel.

---

[5] Preaching Law and Gospel by Herman Stuempfle. Fortress Press, 31.

The Inadequacy of Behavior Modification

The Christian Church loves to preach the Law.

It loves to give us lists, steps, and advice. None of these are necessarily bad things, but they never actually deal with the heart of the problem. Many of our churches have become content with creating well-behaved constituents instead of forgiven children of God.

We say we are saved by grace alone but our conversations, our sermons, and our behavior speaks otherwise. We act as though our relationship with God depends on our ability to do the right things. A friend of mine often says, "We want to have some skin in the game."[6] We cling to our own works with hopes that they might provide some sort of validation or proof that God has done something in us.

---

[6] My friend Daniel Price said this. Check out his ministry ChristHoldFast.org

When the Law is seen as terminal - all God gives us - behavior modification becomes the Savior and our own efforts and intentions become "the Way, the Truth, and the Life."

Think about it, behavior modification is essential to the Christian life. If you're an addict, you need to modify your behavior if you want to live. If you're a bad husband, you need to modify your behavior if you want your marriage to thrive. If you spend your money carelessly, you need to modify your behavior in order to avoid bankruptcy.

Behavior is important. Behavior modification is a practical implementation of the Law into the way we make decisions. But the Law alone won't fix the real problem.

The Law doesn't ultimately exist to change our behavior, although it certainly encourages changed behavior, it exists to lead us to Christ. It exists to eventually lead us to the truth that Jesus comes for the law-breakers not for the law-keepers.

The goal of the Law is repentance. When the Law does it's work we have nowhere to turn but to the cross. The cross brings life. Jesus gives us hope when we've run out of places to put our hope. Our hope is in a one-sided rescue for hopeless sinners.

B.S. Theology

Chapter 3

Author's Note: I realize that the language of this title might be offensive. I encourage you to push through that tension to be encouraged by the beauty of an honest Law-Gospel theology.

It's time to call bull on a theology that dominates Christianity.

Brandon Bennett, in a post on Mockingbird[7], introduced me to a brilliant book by a philosopher Harry Frankfurt that helps us define and describe bull, what he refers to as "humbug."

---

[7] http://www.mbird.com/2015/01/on-bs-and-the-word-of-absolution/

"Humbug is necessarily designed or intended to deceive, that its misrepresentation is not merely inadvertent. In other words, it is deliberate misrepresentation." – Harry Frankfurt[8]

He suggests that those "full of it" deliberately misrepresent the truth. He further suggests that humbug has some similar characteristics to lying but is not always the same. He also states that humbug is not just about the things people say, but can be accompanied, "especially by pretentious word or deed."[9]

Frankfurt describes the bull sh** of a man running off at the mouth during a Fourth of July party. "What he cares about is what people think of him." He doesn't care whether or not what he says is true, he cares that what he says makes him look good. Does this not mimic what we find in the Church - behavior that is more about what others think than what God desires?

---

[8] *On Bullshit* by Harry Frankfurt. Princeton University Press, 6.

[9] Ibid., 18.

Tell me if this seems a bit pretentious:

"Two men went up into the temple to pray, one a Pharisee and the other a tax collector. The Pharisee, standing by himself, prayed thus: 'God, I thank you that I am not like other men, extortioners, unjust, adulterers, or even like this tax collector. I fast twice a week; I give tithes of all that I get.' – Luke 18:9-12

The Pharisees were the well-respected religious leaders of Jesus' days. They were known for the obedience to the law and their teaching of the Scriptures. If there's a picture of godliness for a Jew in the time of Jesus, it's a Pharisee.

Jesus calls out the Pharisees as being full of it. He's caught them - they care more about what people think of them than the reality of their own heart.

And be careful, because if you read this and start thinking, "Yeah, preach to those legalists," you might be one. Because in the boasting of your success or in the boasting of being unlike the boasters - we're all the same.

I am eerily familiar with the attitude Jesus condemns. I spend my time deliberately misrepresenting reality to myself to convince myself that I'm not that bad, whatever "that bad" is. I'm full of it when I justify my own failures and look at others with condemnation because of their own sins. I'm a broken hypocrite who persists in a constant quest to convince myself and the people around me that I'm good enough, that I know enough, and that I'm much better than "those people." I'm better than "those sinners." I'm nothing like "those Christians."

If you don't think you're the Pharisee in Jesus' parable, you probably are.

The Christian who understands the art of Law and Gospel has an honesty theology. It's a theology that lays our cards out on the table - it's honest about our failures, our sins and our inadequacy. And it's a theology that doesn't rely on convincing your peers that your good, but relies on trusting in Jesus as the one who was good on your behalf.

Grace calls B.S. on any theology that focuses more on what you do than what's been done.

Unfortunately, within Christianity there are far too many who live with a theology that's full of it. I know that's crude, but the facade people often create under the guise of Christianity is astonishingly unChristian, and sad.

Jesus' calls the bluff of the Pharisees in Matthew 23:27-28 when he says, "Woe to you, teachers of the law and Pharisees, you hypocrites! You are like whitewashed tombs, which look beautiful on the outside but on the inside are full of the bones of the dead and everything unclean. In the same way, on the outside you appear to people as righteous but on the inside you are full of hypocrisy and wickedness." In other words, Jesus is calling bull.

They might be able to do all the right things. They might be able to vote for the right party, watch only the right movies, and read the right books, but inside they are not as good as they appear to be. What we read as Pharisees in Jesus' day are what we might call legalists in our own. Legalists are those more concerned with their obedience than the work of Christ. Legalists are those who'd rather focus on "doing more" and "trying harder" instead of what's been done for them. Legalism turns away from a message of grace and to a list of rules that determine who's in and who's out.

Legalism is one of the most dangerous confusions of Law and Gospel and the only way of dealing with this problem is calling it what it is.

B.S.

Legalism isn't helpful, it isn't hopeful, and it certainly isn't Christian.

Skubalon

The Apostle Paul recognizes honest theology in Philippians when he writes these words:

"Indeed, I count everything as loss because of the surpassing worth of knowing Christ Jesus my Lord. For his sake I have suffered the loss of all things and count them as rubbish, in order that I may gain Christ." - Philippians 3:8

Paul understands that all our efforts and good intentions result in nothing more than a pile of crap. And Paul actually has stuff he can brag about; in the verses right before this he actually goes on and on just in case we don't know how big a deal he is. If anybody had a track record of piety worth a medal, it was Paul. If anybody could have given the Pharisees a run for their money, it was Paul. If anybody could make the best of the legalists look bad, it was Paul.

And Paul makes sure we know all those things, but then says this about his own merits, "That's all worth nothing."

In fact, the literal translation of this passage is even better. In Greek, Paul says I count all my good works as *skubalon,* that is, excrement. Paul wants us to know that our good intentions and our obedience is worth nothing more than a pile of B.S. Paul calls bull on the false theology that is built on works.

The KJV says it this way:

"I count all things but loss for the excellency of the knowledge of Christ Jesus my Lord: for whom I have suffered the loss of all things, and do count them but dung, that I may win Christ." - Philippians 3:8

May God wreck us with his Word of Law and remind us that we're not as good as we think we are. When the Law does its work, it will make us honest. The Law will cut through the images we've created for ourselves to reveal what's inside. And when the Law truly does its work it makes our prayer the prayer of the tax collector:

"But the tax collector, standing far off, would not even lift up his eyes to heaven, but beat his breast, saying, 'God, be merciful to me, a sinner!' " – Luke 18:13

Grace

"Grace is love that seeks you
out when you have nothing
to give in return...
Grace is being loved when
you are unlovable."

Paul Zahl

I've Got 99 Problems But Karma Ain't One

Chapter 4

The idea that we get what we deserve is an appealing way to look at the world. While some of us might not admit that we actually believe in Karma, many of us believe it without even realizing it. People, regardless of their faith background, like to think that if they do something good, something good will happen in return.

If Karma is true, we're all screwed.

If somebody believes in Karma and believes things are going well for them, they have an arrogant view of themselves. Karma suggests that everybody gets what they deserve. This means that if somebody is rewarded, they get the credit. And if somebody is punished, they get the blame.

If things are going well - if you got the job, the marriage, the house - then you are receiving rewards for what you have done. But if things are going poorly - if you lost your job, your marriage is falling apart, or you have an incurable disease - then you are receiving exactly what you deserve.

In this world nothing happens to a person that he does not for some reason or other deserve. Usually, men of ordinary intellect cannot comprehend the actual reason or reasons. The definite invisible cause or causes of the visible effect is not necessarily confined to the present life, they may be traced to a proximate or remote past birth. - Buddhanet.net

You'd better hope you were really good in your past lives!

This worldview runs totally contrary to the Christian God's message of grace. Grace is the enemy of Karma.

What is grace? Grace is love that seeks you out when you have nothing to give in return. Grace is love coming at you that has nothing to do with you. Grace is being loved when you are unlovable. It is being loved when you are the opposite of lovable. - Paul Zahl[10]

Grace knows what we deserve. And it gives us the opposite. And in the face of things going poorly, grace - instead of trying to answer why - simply promises to be with us in the midst of the pain.

While Karma suggests that we end up damned, grace gives us eternal life. While Karma requires an eye-for-an-eye, grace turns the other cheek. While Karma always balances the scales, grace never stops giving because the scales will never balance (God always gives more). While Karma suggests that it is all about our work, grace suggests that it is all about the work of Jesus.

If Karma were applied as a teaching of Christianity, Karma would be all Law. Karma

---

[10] *Grace in Practice* by Paul Zahl. William B. Eerdmans Publishing Company, 36.

relies on our own effort to add weight to the scale of "good" in our life. Karma relies on our own efforts to justify ourselves with enough good to outweigh the bad.

What if the Apostle Paul believed in Karma?

"None is righteous, no, not one; no one understands; no one seeks for God. All have turned aside; together they have become worthless; no one does good, not even one." - Romans 3:11-12

Paul suggests that if Karma were true, we're all going to hell. This is what makes grace so scandalous to the human mind. We don't get what we deserve. We deserve punishment. We deserve death.

What is Karma's answer to death? Cancer? Divorce? We deserved it. It's punishment.

Grace doesn't play by these rules. Grace is the scandal that never gives us what we deserve and always gives us what we need:

Mercy.

Peace.

Hope.

Joy.

Forgiveness.

The band Relient K once described this by saying, "But the beauty of grace is that it makes life not fair." Grace says what the Law never will. Grace creates beauty, hope, and peace that rests not in our own efforts but in the finished work of Jesus.

Many Christians have become functional Buddhists, trusting in their own works, believing a theology that paints everything within a system of obedience, rewards, and punishment - a system that is often eerily similar to Karma.

This isn't Christianity, it's B.S. This is a Law-based system that gives people false assurance and burdened consciences - exactly what every other religion offers. Every religion besides Christianity is Law-based.

And while the work of the Law is important in Christianity, the Law never has the last word. When the Law gets the last word, we find ourselves crushed and without hope. Grace is the pronouncement of "done" that quiets words that judge.

If people are looking for good Karma - guilt in failure or advice to balance to scales - they can get that anywhere. From Islam to Buddhism to Atheism, "do this" or "don't do this" is the primary message. From the bestseller list to mommy-bloggers, the Law is the default message.

If you're looking for peace, Karma doesn't offer it. If you're looking for hope, Karma doesn't point to it. Mercy? Karma's got nothing.

What you're looking for can be found in the Church. Grace is given freely by the family of God. Jesus gives peace, hope, and mercy and it has nothing to do with obedience, rewards, or punishment.

If you're looking for a perfect Christian church, you won't find one. They're all filled with hypocrites who like to point out other people's sin before their own. They're made up of gossips, liars, and cheaters. Sin does to a church what it does to everyone - it ruins relationships, including in the family of God.

The Church has a lot of problems, but grace ain't one. Grace is the one thing that unites the church. It is the one thing that breaks down barriers between sinners. Every age, every race, and every socio-economic status are united by one thing, "Jesus Christ and him crucified." [11]

If somebody is looking for a self-help program, they aren't going to come to your church - the world offers better ones. If somebody is looking for the structure of a religious life, they have thousands of religions to choose from. In fact, the demands of secular life are difficult enough that most people don't need religion to add to it.

One reason people are running away from Christianity isn't that they have a problem with Jesus, it's because churches aren't

---

[11] 1 Corinthians 2:1-2

preaching the Gospel - they've settled for Karma instead of grace.

There is no place but the Church that forgives with no questions asked. If somebody is a rebel, an outcast, or on the verge of death, the Church of Jesus specializes in the one who comes for the rebels, welcomes in the outcasts, and raises the dead. The death and resurrection sets the Church apart from the world, no one else can offer that to the world, including Buddha.

Grace gets the last word.

"It is finished."

How God Cures Daily Amnesia

Chapter 5

The Journal of Neuroscience records the study of an 84-year-old retired lab technician named E.P. E.P. suffered from one of the most severe cases of amnesia ever documented. He could only recall his most recent thought. Answers to questions like, "Who is the President?" or "What did you have for dinner?" would be completely unknown to him.

In the book *Moonwalking with Einstein*, Joshua Foer describes his encounter with E.P. and the amnesia he suffered. When Joshua met with E.P. they went on a walk. On the walk, the author noticed several different things about E.P. He took the same route every time, yet if you were to ask E.P. to draw the map of his route, he had no idea where he traveled. He found items along the way only to forget where they came from by the time he returned home. As he passed by his neighbors, he reintroduced himself to them every time as though they were complete strangers. E.P.'s neighbors, his street, and even his own house were foreign to him.

And as they approached E.P.'s home, they walked by a car. As they looked in the car's mirror-like tinted window, Joshua asked E.P. "What do you see?" E.P. stared at his reflection and answered, "An old man. That's all."

An old man.

That's all.

When you look in the mirror what do you see?

The Law is a mirror that shows us what we really look like. It tells us the truth about ourself. When I look in a mirror, if I'm honest, I see someone disturbing. I see an adulterer, an addict, a thief, a liar. As I study my face, shame comes rushing back as the reflection says, "This is who you are. That's all."

This is where the problem lies. We are forgetful people. Our short-term memories only go back as far as the reflection of the Law. We remember the shame and the guilt, but we forget the promise. We have a "Gospel Amnesia" that makes us forget who we are in Christ. Our forgetfulness leaves us looking at our reflection like E.P. and seeing only guilt and shame.

This isn't a new problem; God's people have always been forgetful. Rescued people forget they are rescued. Forgiven people forget they are forgiven. In Deuteronomy, when Moses is preaching to the nation of Israel who has been rescued from slavery he gives them an important reminder.

When the Lord your God brings you into the land that he swore to your fathers, to Abraham, to Isaac, and to Jacob, to give you—with great and good cities that you did not build, and houses full of all good things that you did not fill, and cisterns that you did not dig, and vineyards and olive trees that you did not plant—and when you eat and are full, then take care lest you forget the Lord, who brought you out of the land of Egypt. (Deuteronomy 6:10-12 ESV)

The Israelites forget they've been rescued from slavery. The disciples forget the teaching of the Savior they followed. You and I forget the God who calls me his own.

The problem isn't with the mirror revealing what we really look like; the problem is that we forget what Christ says despite what we really look like. The problem is that we forget the very thing we need to remember while we remember the very things we need to forget.

We forget what Paul says in 2 Corinthians 5:17, "If anyone is in Christ, he is a new creation. The old has passed away; behold, the new has come."

And the things we hold onto are the very things that God himself says he forgets.

"I am he who blots out your transgressions for my own sake, and I will not remember your sins." - Isaiah 43:25

There's a fitting story told by Rod Rosenbladt, former professor of theology at Concordia University in Irvine, of a middle-aged woman who approaches her pastor in need of counseling:

She went to her pastor and said, "Pastor, I had an abortion a number of years ago." "OK," the Pastor replied. "Well, I need to talk to you about the man I've since married." "Alright," replied the Pastor.

"Well, we met a while back, and started dating and I thought, I need to tell him about the abortion. But I just couldn't. Then things got more serious between us and I thought, I need to tell him about the abortion. But I just couldn't. A while later we got engaged and I thought, I need to tell him about the abortion. But I just couldn't. Then we got married and I thought, I really need to tell him about the abortion. But I just couldn't. So I needed to talk to someone, Pastor, and you're it."

The Pastor replied, "You know, we have a service for this. Let's go through that together." So they did—a service of confession and absolution.

When they were finished, she said to him, "Thank you, Pastor. Now I think I have the courage to tell my new husband about my abortion."

And the Pastor replied to her, "What abortion?"[12]

What do you need to forget that God himself has already forgotten? What are you holding onto that Christ took away when he went to the cross?

What sins in your life do you need to hear from God himself, "I remember your sins no more" (Hebrews 8:13)? The promise we hear over and over and over again is that we are sons and daughters by the blood of Jesus. As you look into the tinted windows of the car, forgetting what Christ has said of you and

---

[12] This story is describing what many call confession and absolution. The woman makes her confession and the pastor on behalf of Jesus speaks the words of forgiveness to her: https://christiancounseling.com/blog/the-gospel/my-god-he-knoweth-none/

reminded by the Law of your sin, be reminded that God has amnesia.

The sins that own you, he remembers no more. The person you see in the window, God sees as a son or a daughter. His amnesia cures yours. Grace is the promise that your heavenly Father remembers your sins no more.

G. Rand, A.K. Uzer, & Howe

Chapter 6

Satan is the world's best accuser. If he ran a law firm, he'd be its first and most powerful partner. His specialty is accusing and destroying people. Like you.

He never comes to court unprepared. From the moment you're accused, he's prowling around in front of the jury, ready to attack and make his case.

He's got evidence, eyewitnesses, and testimonies to put you away for life. He calls your friends on the stand to testify about your lies and cover-ups. He puts your family on the stand to reveal your weakness before the jury. His evidence submitted before the court and in full public view includes e-mails, voice-mails, and even off-the-record conversations that make you look like a dirtbag.

And The Accuser doesn't stop there. Witnesses for the prosecution continue until you are crushed with guilt and your character is shamed beyond recovery. You're buried under a mountain of evidence and testimony with no way out.

The accused – you – fight to defend yourself. After all, you got yourself into the mess, so you can at least mount a defense to get yourself out. You think about hiring a lawyer, but opt to make your own defense, boldly ignoring the lawyer's axiom, "He who represents himself has a fool for a client." With your back against the wall facing brutal accusations, what other choice do you have? Can anyone really justify your actions better than you? If there's a chance that you will be found innocent, you have the best shot at making it happen.

That's foolishness, though. You're not going to get off, and you know it. The accusations are accurate. You might as well plead guilty. Your efforts to self-justify and refute the evidence are hopeless.

Counter intuitively, it's in this hopelessness that God meets you in the courtroom where Satan has made his airtight case. Jesus arrives as your advocate. You don't have to make a defense.

Revelation 12:10-11 says, "For the accuser of our brothers and sisters, who accuses them before our God day and night, has been hurled down. They triumphed over him by the blood of the Lamb."

1 John 2 says, "But if anybody does sin, we have an advocate with the Father—Jesus Christ, the Righteous One."

Jesus transforms the proceedings by exchanging his innocence for your guilt. He mitigates the charges against you by offering his own life - his active obedience, his sacrificial death, and his victorious resurrection - all on your behalf. This is an unbeatable tactic. The accuser doesn't stand a chance.

The Law says you are clearly guilty, but Jesus gives you a new shot at life, and there's nothing Satan and his team can do to take that from you.

But the accuser is clever. Even after the case is closed, Satan knows exactly the accusations to whisper to cause you to question your innocence. He knows the wounds to reopen. The accuser is an expert abuser of the Law when he brings up forgiven sins. He is an expert in convincing you that your case might be reopened, perhaps by God himself. Maybe God will change his mind? Maybe your sin is too much for even Jesus to cover?

While Satan continues to accuse and sow doubt, the law is the law. There is no double jeopardy in the Kingdom of God. In Romans 8 Paul writes, "Who will bring any charge against those whom God has chosen. It is God who justifies."

When Jesus says, "Not guilty," that is what you are.

The case is closed.

The gavel falls. Court adjourned.

To Law & Gospel Artists

"The distinction between law and gospel is the highest art in Christendom."

Martin Luther

To the Crazy Ones

Chapter 6

Steve Jobs, the innovator that led Apple into greatness, once said:

"Here's to the crazy ones. The misfits. The rebels. The troublemakers. The round pegs in the square holes. The ones who see things differently. They're not fond of rules. And they have no respect for the status quo. You can quote them, disagree with them, glorify or vilify them. About the only thing you can't do is ignore them. Because they change things. They push the human race forward. And while some may see them as the crazy ones, we see genius. Because the people who are crazy enough to think they can change the world, are the ones who do."

When Apple ran this advertising campaign, Steve Jobs was interested in reforming the way that computers were used. He began a movement of misfits and rebels that changed the personal computer forever. His radical innovations forever changed technology.

The Reformation also began with a crazy one. Martin Luther was a misfit and perceived rebel, with no respect for the status quo of the medieval, Roman Catholic church. In a time when the Church had chosen to literally sell forgiveness, Luther made a way forward by calling the Church back to the message of the Gospel. When the medieval church made their money by crushing people with the Law, Luther rebelled by returning to a message that had been forgotten.

Luther was a troublemaker for all the right reasons. He knew he may be foolish, but he was betting it all on God's scandalous message of grace for the undeserving.

Imagine a world where Christians were known for this message. What if Christians were known for the good news instead of political agendas? What if Christians rebelled against the status quo of rules and lists and emphasized the finished work of Jesus? What if Christians were counter-cultural by preaching "it is finished," in a "do more, try harder" world?

We need a Church with Christians crazy enough to bet everything on grace. A Church crazy enough to know nothing "except Jesus Christ and him crucified."[13]

Here's to the crazy ones.

"For the message of the cross is foolishness to those who are perishing, but to us who are being saved it is the power of God."[14] Or in the translation of Steve Jobs, "Stay hungry. Stay foolish."

---

[13] 1 Corinthians 2:2

[14] 1 Corinthians 1:18.

Additional Law & Gospel Resources

William McDavid, Ethan Richardson, and David Zahl, *Law and Gospel: A Theology for Sinners and Saints*. (Charlottesville, VA: Mockingbird Ministries, 2015).

RJ Grunewald, *Galatians: Selections from Martin Luther's Commentary*. (Publisher: Author, 2015).

John Pless, *Handling the Word of Truth: Law and Gospel in the Church Today*. (St. Louis, MO: Concordia Publishing House, 2015).

Paul Zahl, *Grace in Practice: A Theology for Everyday Life*. (Grand Rapids, MI: Wm. B. Eerdmans Publishing Co, 2007).

Jacob Preus, *Just Words*. (St. Louis, MO: Concordia Publishing House, 2000).

CFW Walther, *The Proper Distinction Between Law and Gospel.* (St. Louis, MO: Concordia Publishing House, 1986).

Steven Hein, *The Christian Life: Cross or Glory.* (Irvine, CA: New Reformation Publications, 2015).

Bo Giertz, *Hammer of God.* (Minneapolis, MN: Augsburg Fortress, 2005).

Author Biography

I'm RJ Grunewald. I love doing what God has called me to do. I'm a husband to my wonderful wife, Jessica. I'm a dad to Elijah and Emaline. I also have the privilege to serve as Pastor at Faith Lutheran Church in Troy, Michigan (my wife and I grew up there). I am currently attending Concordia Seminary in St. Louis, Missouri through their Specific Ministry Pastor program.

If you want more from me, check out rjgrune.com.

36758698R00044

Made in the USA
San Bernardino, CA
01 August 2016